The Master Key Net Worth BLUEPRINT VOL.1

The Master Key Net Worth BLUEPRINT VOL.1

Stacey M. Oliver

Olivers Financial Planning Services, LLC ®™

South Carolina

For more resources, please visit https://www.ofpsagency.com

Disclaimer

The advice contained in this guide may not be suitable for everyone. The author obtained information from sources that may be reliable and from her own experience. The information in this guide is provided for education and informational purposes only, without any express or implied warranty of any kind, including warranties of accuracy, completeness for any particular purpose. The material contained in this guide is not intended to be and does not constitute financial, legal or any other advice. The information is general in nature and is not specific to you the user or anyone else. The author, distributor and publisher particularly disclaims any liability, loss or risk taken by individuals who directly or indirectly act on the information contained herein. All readers must accept all and full responsibilities for their use of this material. All pictures used in this guide are for illustrated purposes only. The pictures are only licensed for use of this guide and must not be used for any other purpose without prior written permission of the rights holder.

Copyrights

Work Cited
(https://en.oxforddictionaries.com/, n.d.)
(https://en.wikipedia.org/wiki/, n.d.)
(https://www.merriam-webster.com/, since 1828)

Printed and Published in the United States of America

The Master Key Net Worth BLUEPRINT VOL.1
STACEY M. OLIVER

ISBN-13: 978-1-7350929-1-1

Interior Designs by STACEY M. OLIVER

A New Kind of Agency

Olivers Financial Planning Services, LLC

(aka OFPS, LLC) was incorporated and founded by Stacey M. Oliver, CEO, in 2015. Our mission is to create, enlighten, and empower committed effective stewards of finances. Our primary objective is to increase our clients' financial literacy awareness so they can fully understand how money works.

"Money can work hard for you instead of you working hard for it. Once that concept is learned then the vicious cycle and hold of debt can be removed."

Hello

Hi, I'm ***Stacey M. Oliver***, your Barrier Breaker and Financial Locksmith.

I empower individuals with the Master Key to unlocking doors to financial freedom.

Now let me ask...What is keeping the doors locked to you obtaining total financial freedom? The answer is simple, *Barrier(s).* A barrier is an obstacle that prevents movement, access, or progress.

If you do not become empowered with the Master Key to complete financial freedom the trend of financial barriers and financial ignorance will continue to filter and recycle through you and/or your family.

If the financial barrier is not broken and destroyed in our lives, there will not be a financial legacy left for our next generation. Stop allowing the doors to remain locked to your financial freedom. **Possess the Master Key and start taking charge of unlocking doors to your financial wealth so you can begin to experience Financial FREEDOM.**

Objectives

The Master Key Net Worth Blueprint workbook will increase your financial knowledge base. Understanding your Net Worth is imperative just as knowing yourself.

The **Blueprint** breaks down how to evolve into financial shape and how to set smart goals. In this guide you will learn why it is vital to shift your mind-set to experience a lifestyle of complete financial freedom. This workbook is a key success to your financial success.

RATE YOURSELF
&
SHIFT YOUR FOCUS

"Empowering Individuals with the Master Key to Complete Financial Freedom" -Stacey M. Oliver

Rate Yourself

Circle one for each category with five being strongly agree and one being strongly disagree.

Determined 1 2 3 4 5

(firm decision; adamant; unwavering)

Self-motivated 1 2 3 4 5

(without supervision; initiative to undertake)

Self-discipline 1 2 3 4 5

(overcome one's weaknesses; the ability to make yourself do things that should be done)

Self-control 1 2 3 4 5

(the ability to manage your actions, feelings, and emotions)

Persistent 1 2 3 4 5

(continuing firmly in a course of action in spite of difficulty/opposition; continuing to endure over a prolonged period; preserving; lasting; enduring)

Shift Your Focus

Change your Focus from Poor to Rich.

"Change Your Mindset, Change Your Money."

Poor Focus	Rich Focus
Saying I can't	Saying I can
Just dreaming	Living the dream
Later	Now
Neglecting change	Being the change
Not knowing	Knowing
Doubting	Believing
Hearing only	Doing
Spending	Saving
Being unproductive	Being productive
Improvising	Planning
I don't have	I do have
It won't work	It will work

It's all about *Eradicating* the negativity you have in your mind and *Affirm* it with a **YES**!!!

Shift Your Focus continued...

Declare what you will Stop and Start Today!

(Fill in the boxes under the START column.)

"Financial Freedom is a Language."

STOP	START
Saying I can't	
Just dreaming	
Later	
Neglecting change	
Not knowing	
Doubting	
Hearing only	
Spending	
Being unproductive	
Improvising	
I don't have	
It won't work	

It's all about *Eradicating* the negativity you have in your mind and *Affirm* it with a **YES**!!!

Quick Reminders

FINANCIAL GOALS

"Excellence is not an act. Excellence is a habit. Excellence is what you habitually DO."

-Stacey M. Oliver

Becoming *Financially* Fit

- Do you know your net worth?
- What percentage of your income goes to retirement?
- Do you have a WILL?
- Do you have 3 – 6 months of living income stashed?
- Is your family protected?
- Do you know your credit score?
- Have you obtained and reviewed your credit report lately?
- Do you have emergency funds?
- Do you have or maintain a budget system?
- Do you find yourself spending more than you make?

GOALS

Growing your money with an open mind and exploring alternatives for long-term savings.

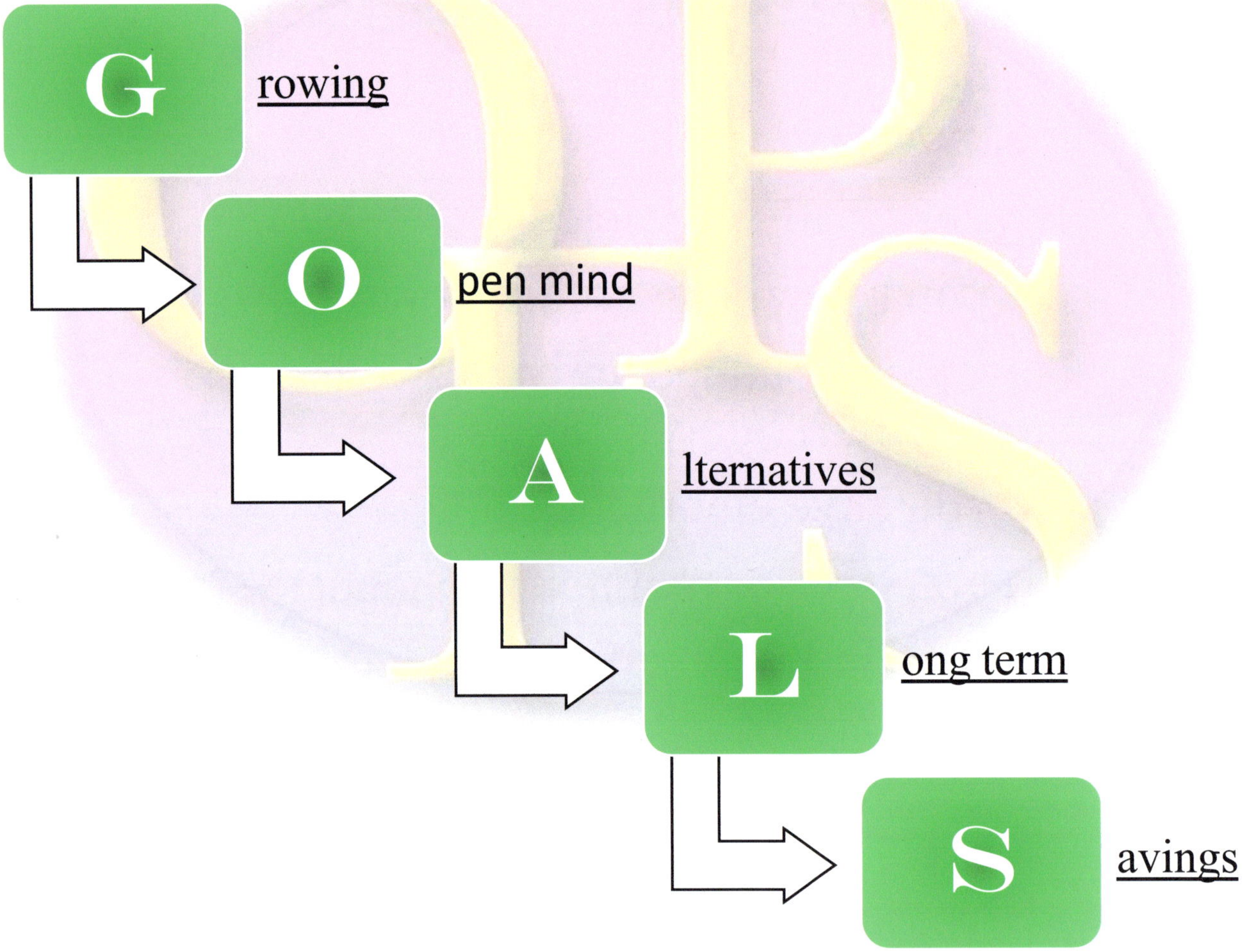

Financial Goals

- Brainstorm and picture your next 12 months or perhaps the next 10 years. Are you on the right track to meeting your financial goals or do you need to reset and make some changes?
- Determine an Outcome. Do you need to payoff some debt or pay down some debt? Do you need to increase your savings? Do you need to curtail your spending?
- Compose an attainable goal to payoff debt/pay down and/or increase savings.
- Analyze your goal and make sure it makes sense and it is attainable.
  - a) The length of time it will take to meet goal.
  - b) The cost factor (*the total amount of money needed*).
- Track your progress. Are you on your way to meeting goal?
- Keep going and complete your goal.
- Celebrate each milestone. Rather focusing on how much longer or how much more…focus on the outcome and the progress. Every minor step gets you to the major step. Focusing on the outcome keeps you motivated.
- Once goal is met, mark accomplishment.

Timeline worksheets have been provided to track your goals.

Financial Goals Timeline

Timeline

Brainstorm → Determine Outcome → Compose a Goal → Analyze Goal → Track Goal → Complete Goal → Conclude w/date of Completion

	Complete By MM/DD/YYYY	Action Plan
☐		
☐		
☐		
☐		
☐		
☐		
☐		
☐		
☐		
☐		

Financial Goals Timeline

Timeline

Brainstorm → Determine Outcome → Compose a Goal → Analyze Goal → Track Goal → Complete Goal → Conclude w/date of Completion

	Complete By MM/DD/YYYY	Action Plan
☐		
☐		
☐		
☐		
☐		
☐		
☐		
☐		
☐		
☐		

For more resources, please visit https://www.ofpsagency.com

Financial Goals Timeline

Timeline

Brainstorm → Determine Outcome → Compose a Goal → Analyze Goal → Track Goal → Complete Goal → Conclude w/date of Completion

	Complete By MM/DD/YYYY	Action Plan
☐		
☐		
☐		
☐		
☐		
☐		
☐		
☐		
☐		
☐		

Financial Goals Timeline

Timeline

Brainstorm → Determine Outcome → Compose a Goal → Analyze Goal → Track Goal → Complete Goal → Conclude w/date of Completion

	Complete By MM/DD/YYYY	Action Plan
☐		
☐		
☐		
☐		
☐		
☐		
☐		
☐		
☐		
☐		

Financial Goals Timeline

Timeline

Brainstorm → Determine Outcome → Compose a Goal → Analyze Goal → Track Goal → Complete Goal → Conclude w/date of Completion

	Complete By MM/DD/YYYY	Action Plan
☐		
☐		
☐		
☐		
☐		
☐		
☐		
☐		
☐		
☐		

For more resources, please visit https://www.ofpsagency.com

Financial Goals Timeline

Timeline

Brainstorm → Determine Outcome → Compose a Goal → Analyze Goal → Track Goal → Complete Goal → Conclude w/date of Completion

	Complete By MM/DD/YYYY	Action Plan
☐		
☐		
☐		
☐		
☐		
☐		
☐		
☐		
☐		
☐		

For more resources, please visit https://www.ofpsagency.com

Quick Reminders

NET WORTH

"Are you ready to make the decision to change your financial status? Complete financial freedom is attainable." -Stacey M. Oliver

Net Worth

Knowing your **Net Worth** is a simple equation:

ASSETS — LIABILITIES = NET WORTH

Net worth represents the properties owned, less any debt an individual has.

Net Worth

Net Worth	Bad	Good
What is your current life cash value? If you have more assets (own) than liabilities (owe), you have a positive net worth. If you do not, you have a negative net worth in other words no monetary cash value. **Assets/Own – Liab./Owe** = **Net Worth**	Debt > Income Expenses > Income Assets < Liabilities	Debt < Income Expenses < Income Assets > Liabilities

> **Greater than** **or** **<** **Less than**

Net Worth

If your out of pocket expenses are more than your take home pay, here are some options to consider:

- **Set, Start and Stick to Budget**
- **Eliminate Unnecessary Debt**
- **Debt Consolidation**
- **Refinance**

"Money wasted is Money not well spent."

Test Your Knowledge

Net Worth is an individual's total assets of what's owned minus total liabilities or expenses of what's owed.

- ❑ True
- ❑ False

❑ True Correct Answer

Net Worth

Calculate your **Net Worth** by completing the worksheet on the next few pages. A sample sheet has been provided for your guidance.

Extra worksheets have been provided to recalculate your net worth as you payoff debt and increase your assets, cash savings and/or investments.

NET WORTH

DATE: MM/DD/YYYY

ASSETS (OWN)		LIABILITIES (OWE)	
Personal Items	Estimated Value	Outstanding Debt/Loan Balances	Estimated Value
Home	205,000	Mortgage	150,000
Vacation Home		2nd Mortgage (Home Equity)	
Real Estate Property		Real Estate	
Automobiles	1,100	Automobiles	58,321
Motor Home		Student Loan	85,200
Boats		Finance Companies	6,609
Jewelry		Other Loans	
Fur			
Furniture		Other Debt	
Electronics		Credit Card Debt	10,200
Antiques	17,050	Other Debt	
Live Stocks			
Other Assts			
Cash or Equivalent to Cash			
Checking	400		
Savings	3,180		
CD's	500		
Money Market			
Life Insurance w/Cash Value (excluding Term)			
Other			
Investments			
Retirement (401K, IRA, Traditional IRS)	215,640		
Bonds			
Mutual Funds			
Individual Stock Shares			
Real Estate Property ((excluding Home)			
Other			
Total Assets	$442,870	Total LIABILITIES	$310,330
Estimated Net Worth:	$132,540		

SAMPLE

Is your mindset serving as a barrier against your absolute economic power. – **Stacey M Oliver**

NET WORTH

DATE:______________________________

ASSETS (OWN)		LIABILITIES (OWE)	
Personal Items	Estimated Value	Outstanding Debt/Loan Balances	Estimated Value
Home		Mortgage	
Vacation Home		2nd Mortgage (Home Equity)	
Real Estate Property		Real Estate	
Automobiles		Automobiles	
Motor Home		Student Loan	
Boats		Finance Companies	
Jewelry		Other Loans	
Fur			
Furniture		Other Debt	
Electronics		Credit Card Debt	
Antiques		Other Debt	
Live Stocks			
Other Assts			
Cash or Equivalent to Cash			
Checking			
Savings			
CD's			
Money Market			
Life Insurance w/Cash Value (excluding Term)			
Other			
Investments			
Retirement (401K, IRA, Traditional IRS)			
Bonds			
Mutual Funds			
Individual Stock Shares			
Real Estate Property ((excluding Home)			
Other			
Total Assets	$	Total LIABILITIES	$
Estimated Net Worth: $			

Is your mindset serving as a barrier against your absolute economic power. – **Stacey M Oliver**

NET WORTH

DATE:______________________________

ASSETS (OWN)		LIABILITIES (OWE)	
Personal Items	Estimated Value	Outstanding Debt/Loan Balances	Estimated Value
Home		Mortgage	
Vacation Home		2nd Mortgage (Home Equity)	
Real Estate Property		Real Estate	
Automobiles		Automobiles	
Motor Home		Student Loan	
Boats		Finance Companies	
Jewelry		Other Loans	
Fur			
Furniture		Other Debt	
Electronics		Credit Card Debt	
Antiques		Other Debt	
Live Stocks			
Other Assts			
Cash or Equivalent to Cash			
Checking			
Savings			
CD's			
Money Market			
Life Insurance w/Cash Value (excluding Term)			
Other			
Investments			
Retirement (401K, IRA, Traditional IRS)			
Bonds			
Mutual Funds			
Individual Stock Shares			
Real Estate Property ((excluding Home)			
Other			
Total Assets	$	Total LIABILITIES	$
Estimated Net Worth: $			

Is your mindset serving as a barrier against your absolute economic power. – **Stacey M Oliver**

NET WORTH

DATE:______________________________

ASSETS (OWN)		LIABILITIES (OWE)	
Personal Items	Estimated Value	Outstanding Debt/Loan Balances	Estimated Value
Home		Mortgage	
Vacation Home		2nd Mortgage (Home Equity)	
Real Estate Property		Real Estate	
Automobiles		Automobiles	
Motor Home		Student Loan	
Boats		Finance Companies	
Jewelry		Other Loans	
Fur			
Furniture		Other Debt	
Electronics		Credit Card Debt	
Antiques		Other Debt	
Live Stocks			
Other Assts			
Cash or Equivalent to Cash			
Checking			
Savings			
CD's			
Money Market			
Life Insurance w/Cash Value (excluding Term)			
Other			
Investments			
Retirement (401K, IRA, Traditional IRS)			
Bonds			
Mutual Funds			
Individual Stock Shares			
Real Estate Property ((excluding Home)			
Other			
Total Assets	$	Total LIABILITIES	$

Estimated Net Worth: $

Is your mindset serving as a barrier against your absolute economic power. – **Stacey M Oliver**

NET WORTH

DATE:______________________________________

ASSETS (OWN)		LIABILITIES (OWE)	
Personal Items	Estimated Value	Outstanding Debt/Loan Balances	Estimated Value
Home		Mortgage	
Vacation Home		2nd Mortgage (Home Equity)	
Real Estate Property		Real Estate	
Automobiles		Automobiles	
Motor Home		Student Loan	
Boats		Finance Companies	
Jewelry		Other Loans	
Fur			
Furniture		Other Debt	
Electronics		Credit Card Debt	
Antiques		Other Debt	
Live Stocks			
Other Assts			
Cash or Equivalent to Cash			
Checking			
Savings			
CD's			
Money Market			
Life Insurance w/Cash Value (excluding Term)			
Other			
Investments			
Retirement (401K, IRA, Traditional IRS)			
Bonds			
Mutual Funds			
Individual Stock Shares			
Real Estate Property ((excluding Home)			
Other			
Total Assets	$	Total LIABILITIES	$

Estimated Net Worth: $

Is your mindset serving as a barrier against your absolute economic power. – **Stacey M Oliver**

NET WORTH

DATE:______________________________

ASSETS (OWN)		LIABILITIES (OWE)	
Personal Items	Estimated Value	Outstanding Debt/Loan Balances	Estimated Value
Home		Mortgage	
Vacation Home		2nd Mortgage (Home Equity)	
Real Estate Property		Real Estate	
Automobiles		Automobiles	
Motor Home		Student Loan	
Boats		Finance Companies	
Jewelry		Other Loans	
Fur			
Furniture		Other Debt	
Electronics		Credit Card Debt	
Antiques		Other Debt	
Live Stocks			
Other Assts			
Cash or Equivalent to Cash			
Checking			
Savings			
CD's			
Money Market			
Life Insurance w/Cash Value (excluding Term)			
Other			
Investments			
Retirement (401K, IRA, Traditional IRS)			
Bonds			
Mutual Funds			
Individual Stock Shares			
Real Estate Property ((excluding Home)			
Other			
Total Assets	$	Total LIABILITIES	$
Estimated Net Worth: $			

Is your mindset serving as a barrier against your absolute economic power. – **Stacey M Oliver**

ACCOUNT LOG SHEET

"Unlock the door of your mind with the key of KNOWLEDGE."–Stacey M. Oliver

Account Log

	WEBSITE LINK	ACCOUNT#	*USERNAME*	*PASSWORD*
LOANS				
EXAMPLE: World Finance	https://www.loansbyworld.com/	987456321	JonDoe1	3JoN!Do3
CREDIT CARDS/LINE OF CREDIT				
UTILITIES				
AUTO INSURANCE				

For more resources, please visit https://www.ofpsagency.com

Account Log

	WEBSITE LINK	ACCOUNT#	*USERNAME*	*PASSWORD*
LOANS				
CREDIT CARDS/LINE OF CREDIT				
UTILITIES				
AUTO INSURANCE				

Account Log *continued...*

	WEBSITE LINK	ACCOUNT#	*USERNAME*	*PASSWORD*
PERSONAL BANK ACCOUNTS				
BUSINESS BANK ACCOUNTS				
INVESTMENTS AND RETIREMENT				
LIFE INSURANCE				

At-A-Glance

TAKE ACTION

Take Action

TO DO LIST

Priority	Due Date	What	Who	In Progress	Done

NOTES:

TO DO LIST

Priority	Due Date	What	Who	In Progress	Done

NOTES:

Take Action

TO DO LIST

Priority	Due Date	What	Who	In Progress	Done

NOTES:

Take Action

TO DO LIST

Priority	Due Date	What	Who	In Progress	Done

NOTES:

Stay Connected

Olivers Financial Planning Services, LLC
(aka OFPS, LLC)

www.ofpsagency.com

https://instagram.com/oliversfps

http://www.twitter.com/Ofpsllc

http://www.facebook.com/Oliversfps

Olivers Financial Planning Services, LLC ®TM

PO Box 51363
Piedmont, SC 29673
Email: ofpsagency@outlook.com

Made in the USA
Monee, IL
05 November 2026

67384875R00036